INTERNAL
CONSULTA
IN HEALTH
SETTING

INTERNAL CONSULTATION IN HEALTH CARE SETTINGS

Robert Bor
Riva Miller

Foreword by
David Campbell & Ros Draper

Systemic Thinking and Practices Series
Series Editors
David Campbell & Ros Draper

Karnac Books
London **1991** New York

First published in 1990 by D.C. Publishing

This edition published in 1991 by H. Karnac (Books) Ltd. 58, Gloucester Road, London SW7 4QY

Distributed in the United States of America by
Brunner/Mazel, Inc.
19, Union Square West,
New York, NY 10003

Typeset by P. Hayes

ISBN 1 85575 020 1

A CIP catalogue record for this book is available from the British Library.

Printed in Great Britain by BPCC Wheatons Ltd, Exeter

Authors

Robert Bor: C. Psychol; AFBPsS; Churchill Fellow. Principal Clinical Psychologist, District AIDS counsellor and Family Therapist, Royal Free Hospital and Hampstead Health District. Honorary Lecturer in the Academic Departments of Medicine and Psychiatry, Royal Free Hospital School of Medicine, London. Member of the Institute of Family Therapy, London.

Riva Miller: BA; SocSci; MSW; Senior Medical Social Worker and Family Therapist, Haemophilia Centre and Haemostasis Unit, and AIDS Counselling Co- ordinator, Royal Free Hospital and Hampstead Health District London. Honorary Senior Lecturer in the Academic Department of Haematology, Royal Free Hospital School of Medicine, London. Consultant, North London Blood Transfusion Centre. Member of the Institute of Family Therapy, London

Acknowledgements

We would like to thank the following people who, in particular, have contributed directly or indirectly to the ideas set out in this book:

David Campbell, Ros Draper, Jonathan Elford, Peter Lang, Caroline Lindsey, Martin Little, Isobel Scher, Peter Speck, Ricky Snyders and Heather Salt.

We are also indebted to Marion Benn, Elizabeth Boyd and Lorraine Campbell who helped with the preparation of the manuscript.

Note
Professionals and patients are usually referred to as 'he' in this book. This does not reflect any bias on the part of the authors but is merely a convenient pronoun.

Editors' Foreword

A s the world and large organisations, become more interconnected, more complex; it becomes impossible to provide a service without considering the way that the service is affected by impinging ideas, activities and relationships. It is becoming more important for any service or project within any large organisation, such as a hospital, to have the benefit of some understanding of the way the service, as one part, fits into the larger whole; as a result professionals who used to simply service providers are now increasingly being asked to be consultants. That is to offer a bird's eye view of what's going on within the complex organisation. This demand has created a new role for professionals in organisations: Internal consultation.

This book by Robert Bor and Riva Miller is very topical. We find there is an increasing demand for consultants skills without the commensurate body of knowledge or training courses to prepare professionals properly for their new role. We are very pleased to be able to publish this book at this time because it will make an important contribution to a growing field.

One of the book's most exciting contributions is the way in which it describes specific problems of hospital service (and in this case some of them are related to AIDS counselling) and then draws the reader back to think about the meaning which specific problems may have in a larger process of the workings of the hospital.

The authors spell out a consultation approach based on family systems thinking, which has proven effective in their setting, yet it can be applied by any professional worker in many different settings. Indeed the book ends with exercises designed for workers to further develop their own consultation skills.

We feel the book will enable the reader to learn how to function within the bureaucracy of their own organisation regardless of the specific problems he or she is facing. Being part of the system affects the way we behave and the way we see the problems before us, but here the reader will find ways of thinking which will allow him to observe himself as part of the system and from this vantage point work more effectively within the organisation.

This book is unusual in another way. No matter how much thinking is done, one eventually wants to know what to do.

Here, the reader will find various checklists in the book can be used to develop new practices but these lists will also change the thinking which the reader brings to bear on requests for internal consultation.

David Campbell,
Ros Draper,
London.
May, 1990

CONTENTS

contents

INTRODUCTION

Alice: *Would you tell me, please which way I ought to go from here?*

Cheshire Cat: *That depends on a good deal on where you want to get to.*

Lewis Carroll

This book sets out to describe how a 'consultant'[1] in a hospital setting can be used to help define and clarify problems, and thus help towards their resolution. Consultation to colleagues in the same organisation is a special professional situation which is common in health care settings. The unique feature of internal consultation is the relationship between the consultant (the person/s offering consultation) and the consultee (the person/s being consulted to) which adds a new dimension to the consultation process. Some of the unique and specific issues and dilemmas that arise from these consultations are described in this book.

1: "Consultant" is an unfortunate choice of word in the UK because it has connotations of an expert medical practitioner advising a patient and providing leadership in a health care team. Consultation in the organisational and interpersonal context implies conversations about problems with a view to problem-resolution and change. The consultant is not necessarily hierarchically superior to the consultee. The term "consultant" or "consultation" is not intended to reflect a medical model view of change.

Readers who are unfamiliar with hospital settings, or indeed with consultation, may wonder: What is consultation? Who are consultants? How do they become consultants? What do consultants actually do when presented with a problem? Although the field of professional consultation is developing and there are now many books and journal articles of relevance, there are many different answers to some of the above questions. Our answers to them have evolved over time and are derived from our own clinical experience from working in a district general hospital which is also a teaching hospital.

One rarely sets out to be a consultant. Instead, experience over time, seniority and shifts in relationships with colleagues may lead to requests for consultation. The ideas about consultation developed from our experience of setting up and running a hospital-based AIDS counselling service. What guided in this task, despite our different professional backgrounds (clinical psychology and social work) was our shared ideas about problem-solving, which are derived from Family-Systems theory and practice. Some of this theory will be described further on in the book. The task of setting up a new service within an existing organisational structure presented opportunities to meet with a wider range of medical nursing and professional managerial staff in the hospital. The contact was usually at two levels. This was in relation to:

a. clinical matters concerning a particular patient; for example, to help grieving parents mourn the loss of their son, and

b. organisational matters that emerged from the clinical work; for example, to teach other professional staff some of the skills required in AIDS counselling.

These two levels are closely linked. Clinical interventions have an impact on one's work in terms of how others define the task of the clinician, how they may choose to evaluate it, how they may view the development of that particular service, and so on. The internal consultant may be called on to address either a clinical or an organisational problem, but in effect, both of these levels must always be addressed.

Why do professional colleagues seek consultation? Problems at work are as inevitable as problems in ones' personal life. Requests for consultation stem from an idea that there is a dilemma or need for specialist discussion about a problem. Consultation begins when someone affected by a problem discusses the difficulty with someone else, be it in a formal consultation setting, over the telephone after seeing a difficult case, in a ward meeting, or in any other setting. Problems, on the other hand, begin when someone first has the idea that there is a problem. It is the activity of discussing a problem, rather than where this takes place and for how long, that defines consultation. The task of the internal consultant is similar in many respects to that of the external consultant, that is someone from outside of the hospital who is called in to consult over some work. The main difference is the relationship between the consultant and the consultee. This can present a series of dilemmas in the consultation, as revealed in the following example:

A psychologist in a general hospital was asked by a doctor to offer on going consultation to an oncology team because it was considered that the team worked in a stressful field and that consultation would raise staff morale. One of the dilemmas faced by members of the oncology team was that should morale improve, they would be expected to provide more psychological support to the patients in the unit and they would require additional time and skills to do this. The consultant psychologist, on the other hand, had already been offering a support service to some patients. For this reason the psychologist had some views about staff relationships in the oncology unit and was aware that not all of the nurses or doctors wanted to become involved in patient support and counselling. The dilemma for the psychologist was, that he had been asked by the head of the oncology unit to consult to the group. A reluctance to become involved in the management of problems between members of professional staff may ultimately result in fewer referrals being made to him which might also impede in the research project in the oncology unit which he was hoping to pursue.

It is helpful to have a model for providing consultation from within one's own organisation in order to deal with this and similar problems. Some ideas about what prompts a request for consultation will be reviewed. A model for internal consultation will be described and the salient features of a Family-Systems approach, which has organized and facilitated our own thinking about consultation, will be highlighted. Case examples are described (which have been disguised in order to preserve the confidential nature of clinical material). Finally, some exercises have been included at the end of the book which are designed to help readers to introduce some of the ideas about consultation into their own work setting and to develop specific skills in relation to the consultation task.

We shall describe our experience of how we set about providing consultation and how we have attempted to solve some of the problems we faced. This is not to suggest that consultation can be taught as a process of 'what-to-say-when'. Clinician, health service managers and other staff who work in the hospital setting will develop their own solutions to problems and challenges. Some of the ideas described in this book may help others to reflect on their own consultation practice and increase the range of approaches and ideas that they bring to their consultation work.

HOW A NEED ARISES FOR INTERNAL CONSULTATION

There is probably no consensus among hospital-based professionals about the use of consultants in relations to problem-solving. Not every problem requires consultation. Conversely, some teams in hospitals arrange for regular and on going consultation in order to prevent day-to-day difficulties from becoming major problems. Difficulties may emerge in working groups when there is an apparent inability to solve a problem, respond to changes or there is a lack of agreement over strategies for problem-solving. In the hospital setting, most problems inevitably have an impact on health service managers in addition to clinical staff because of the hierarchical structure of the organisation through which account-ability is arranged. One implication of this is that the internal consultant should address the wider implications of problems and solutions, and he should not limit his view of the problem to the scenario which the consultee had described. The ability to add a new dimension to a dilemma or to shift people's views about a problem is the basis of successful consultation. New ideas are introduced by making complex issues appear more simple, and by adding complexity to seemingly straightforward issues.

Through the course of consultations, for example, a junior

doctor came to understand that, more than anything else, his career promotion was being held up because he did not pay sufficient attention to the impression he made on his colleagues. He was consistently late for ward meetings, he never wore a tie and he had long hair. This was frowned upon in the conservative teaching hospital. His own explanations for the difficulties he faced in his career progression were in relation to how colleagues on the ward were apparently 'sabotaging his work.' Once he accepted the idea about paying attention to his personal presentation, the impression he made on others changed and he was accepted as a registrar three months later. Problems with his colleagues and his clinical work were no longer an issue requiring discussion.

What Prompts a Request for Consultation Within the Hospital?

Problems emerge when there is a lack of agreement or consensus over an issue or idea. A theory of the formation, maintenance and resolution for problems in human systems has been described by Watzlawick, Weakland and Fisch, (1974). Often when consultation is requested it is highly likely that the individual or team requesting the consultation have the view of being in a 'losing team' in relation to someone else or another department. The need for consultation can therefore be prompted by a need to redress this in order to be seen to be more competent or better placed in the hospital hierarchy. A common practice when seeking consolation is to look outside of the organisation for a consultant or consulting team. This derives from a belief that an outside team is more likely to be impartial and neutral with respect to problems and, as in psychotherapy, this is considered a necessary component of sound clinical practice. There are many advantages to seeking consultation from outside of the organisation, including the idea of impartiality. However, in some situations it may be neither possible (eg cost) nor desirable (eg highly confidential information) for people outside of the organisation, and indeed the unit, to become involved. It is therefore helpful to consider the possible reasons for the request and to formulate ideas about the 'real' problem.

Over time, we have developed a list of possible explanations for request for internal consultation:

Why is the Request for Internal Consultation Being Made?

* The team secretly want to relinquish responsibility for a case or problem and pass it on to the consultation team or another team.

* The problem is apparently 'highly confidential' and there may be fear that 'dirty washing' would be displayed to competitors.

* The experience and expertise of the consultant is valued.

* An internal consultant might be more flexible about time, availability and may be more accessible.

* There may be a belief that there would be greater loyalty and support if the consultant is from within the hospital.

* The consultee may feel de-skilled by a colleague in the context of work matters over which they liaise. The consultee may then feel under pressure to seek 'expert' advice or consultation from the colleague.

* The consultee may experience feeling isolated in the hospital and consultant may create a new connection or relationship. There may be the belief that there is strength in numbers.

* It may be more helpful to have someone in greater authority in the organisation to confirm or reinforce a view or idea or offer a different view.

Consultation is requested and occurs not only when there is a problem but also when people in a healthy system (team) are ready for more growth. Problems that typically prompt a request for consultation in the hospital setting stem from one of three possibilities, even though they may be linked. These are listed below:

Definition of Problem	Example
1. With patients	A medical specialist asked for advice from the consultation liaison psychiatrist about how to

manage a patient who would not comply with treatment.

2. With colleagues

An academic department in a medical school was constantly overlooked when it came to developing and expanding input into the undergraduate curriculum. During a staff meeting there was agreement that some help was needed in finding ways of getting senior colleagues in other departments to see and accept the relative importance of their subject in the medical curriculum.

3. With managers

Moves to privatize some of the services in the mental health unit in a hospital led to staff dissatisfaction with the appointment of new heads of the occupational therapy and psychiatric nursing specialities. Staff felt a hidden agenda for the new appointees was to rationalize the services in preparation for job cuts. The new appointees sought consultation with hospital managers in order to address their concern about the secret tasks linked to their jobs.

There are many other examples of consultation work described in other chapters. It is appropriate however to first discuss some ideas about the consultant and his task.

Who are Internal Consultants and how do they become Consultants?

There are probably very few people who are employed as

organisational consultants in hospitals. On the other hand, many members of staff, particularly those in more senior positions, have in their job descriptions a clause which includes 'consulting to colleagues ...' In effect, this means: talk to and liaise with other staff within the department or outside of it. In some cases, the range of people consulted to is set out in a list. Internal consultants usually have responsibility for clinical or managerial work and undertake consultation in addition to or as part of their job. The following are five attributes of internal consultants. Their consultation work may have resulted from any one or combination of these:

* **Seniority**: in a position within the hospital.

* **Authority**: he is regarded as a specialist in a particular field or in relation to certain problems.

* **Experience**: he has previous experience of successfully dealing with similar problems.

* **Position**: he is in a strategic position, such as the infection control specialist.

* **Personal style**: he is respected for his impartiality, calmness and clear thinking.

While senior members of staff are usually expected to consult to and liaise with colleagues, the consultee may not be under any special obligation to seek consultation. For this reason, one's reputation for good consultation work in the hospital is important. The choice of consultant may be determined by the nature of the problem or the range of available consultants. A senior nurse who is concerned about the spread of hepatitis on a ward is most likely to consult with an infection control specialist. On the other hand, a psychologist having difficulty interviewing an alcoholic patient may seek help from a range of colleagues, including psychiatrists, social workers, occupational therapists and the clergy.

Consultation is a skill that is not usually formally taught in universities or health settings. Professionals may be expected to acquire the relevant skills through adopting the approach and style of colleagues. Increasingly, there are courses available on consultation which are designed to reflect on the consultation task, develop special skills and in some cases provide for consultations of consultation work. Initiation into consultancy work in the health service is usually through experience of problem solving with colleagues. This may lead to requests for 'supervision' or case discussion. The typical opening scenario from a colleague seeking consultation may be: "Can I discuss a clinical case with you?" or, "I'm having some difficulty writing-up my proposal for more staff nurses on the ward. Would you have a look at my draft proposal?" There can be several tiers or levels in consultation. Discussion with colleagues about the consultation work one is engaged in can also take place.

Two central points underpin consultation: how relationships are defined between colleagues and the idea of the hospital as an organisation. These are described below.

Defining Relationships through Consultation

Consultation in the form of discussion or review of a case provides an opportunity for new views to emerge and for some relationships to be redefined. This is not to suggest that every piece of clinical work should be preceded by extensive consultation in relation to the task and outcome. This may be neither warranted nor practical. *It is important, however, for the consultant in the hospital setting to be clear about the nature of his relationship with the consultee: that is, who is clinically responsible for the case.* There is a difference between a referral and a request for consultation over a clinical case. The internal consultant might move between these positions several times a day in relation to a case. The 'consultant' position must therefore be mutually defined. By this we mean, the consultee requests consultation and the consultant agrees to consult. Strictly speaking, this does not always happen in this way. A colleague may, for example, refer a case and the consultant may choose to consult his colleague about how he can develop his work with the patient rather than take on the case himself. This is described in more detail in Chapter 7. Essentially, there must be agreement between the professionals that consultation will take place. As the consultant may move between different positions he needs to be flexible, adaptive and able to 'observe' himself in different interactive positions. There are many different consultation positions, some of which are listed below:

Between Colleagues	A doctor asks a medical colleague working in the same team for

some advice about how to break 'bad news' to a patient.

Between Units/Departments   Members of staff on the Intensive Care Unit request consultation for bereavement issues from the hospital chaplain

Between hospitals   Senior members of staff in an AIDS unit are engaged in consultation with colleagues in another district hospital who are in the process of setting up an AIDS unit in their own hospital.

While the consultant task remains the same in each, the internal consultant will have different relationships with a range of people, depending where they are in the hospital hierarchy. A social worker acting as a consultant to a medical specialist is different to two nurses consulting to one another over a case. Similarly there are differences in relationships if one is consulting to a colleague in the same department, in another part of the hospital or in another hospital altogether. There is a tendency to be more formalised about setting up and conducting the consultation the further one is socially, hierarchically or physically (in terms of localisation) from the consultee.

The Hospital as an Organisation

A Family-Systems approach has been chosen as a theoretical basis in this book from which the internal consultant can work. The reason for choosing this approach is that a large institution such as a hospital has many similarities to a family insofar as the way problems evolve and the way they can be solved. In the hospital setting, for example, a person may react to a particular problem in such a way as to exacerbate the problem. They may seek allies (and thereby create enemies), become ill, act in a more autocratic way, leave the department, and so on. Similar processes can be observed in families confronted with problems. A hospital comprises many departments and disciplines. This inevitably leads to people having different views with departments and between the hospital and other institutions. These differences may stem from a number of sources, including:

a. Models of Care

Doctors may follow a medical model of investigation, diagnosis and treatment of the individual patient. A nurse, on the other hand, may focus on caring for the patient's physical comfort and on his social well being.

b. Hierarchies

Traditionally, the doctor has been viewed as the leader of the health care team and nurses would not normally take initiative without consulting the doctor. There can also be conflicts between managers, who may control finances, and the medical director of a unit.

c. Training

Different professions teach different tasks. Surgeons, for example are valued more for their dexterity and fine motor skills, rather than their ability to communicate well with patients.

d. Generations

There may be tensions between different generations of health care workers which may stem from differences in training. There may be tensions between those who have recently entered into the hospital system and those who have worked there for many years.

In a similar way, a family is made up of generations, and individuals within the family may have different views. Members of the family may also have different roles resulting from hierarchical structures which can also be a source of tension. A Family-Systems model of consultation, as described in the next two chapters, draws out the associations between family and organizational interactional process. This approach is used as a guide for planning the different stages of internal consultation in the hospital.

THE PROCESS OF INTERNAL CONSULTATION

PART 1

PLANNING THE CONSULTATION

There are many approaches that can be used when consulting to professional colleagues. An aim of consultation is to elicit and address different views of problems and to generate a climate in which new ideas, beliefs, alternatives, meanings and behaviours can emerge. There is no research at present which has established the efficacy of any one consultation approach. If the consultation is to be conducted in a professional manner then guide-lines, based on theory of practice, can be used to focus on the different stages of the process and for *conducting the consultation interview*. The guidelines have emerged from a theory of the evolution, maintenance and resolution of interpersonal problems. A *theory* is important because it *informs our professional practice*. Explanations about what happens in clinical practice (ie why a specific intervention was chosen or why another was ruled out) take place between colleagues and between professionals and their students. In some circumstances, explanations have to be made in a court of law. One cannot *not* have an explanation for what happens in clinical practice. In this chapter, one approach is described which has been found to be helpful in expanding to requests for consultation. Such guide-lines help to organize ideas about how to best help colleagues by clarifying roles and professional relationships, and identifying what happens in the course of consultation.

A Family-Systems approach provides a 'map' for problem identification and resolution. The term 'family' and 'system' suggest human interaction and a multiplicity of views, rather than an individualistic model of behaviour. The essential features of a Family-Systems approach are:

1. Behaviour and problems occur in a *context*. That is, they should be examined and understood in the milieu in which they arise.

2. There is *reciprocity* in *relationships*. If something happens to one individual or department in the hospital, it will in turn affect other people in other departments. The resolution of staffing problems may, for example, create a new problem for the finance department which may be under pressure to increase salaries.

3. Relationships between people (whether they are family members or colleagues) are punctuated by *beliefs* and *behaviours*. New ideas or beliefs can lead to different behaviours and vice verse. Belief systems connote apparent consensus and usually evolve over a period of time. There may be, for example, a belief that junior members of staff in a department should not participate in case discussions, or a belief that competition between members of staff in the same department should not be tolerated. These beliefs may have their origins in the 'family' interactional process of staff members or they may be 'inherited' from more senior staff. Problems may arise when beliefs are challenged, through internal or external events such as the appointment of a new staff member or the development of new working practices and operational policies.

4. Problems may occur *at particular developmental stages* in the growth of the hospital, unit or department. Similarly, as in families, problems are most likely to arise at points of change or transition, such as when children are born, when young adults prepare to leave home and when a family member becomes ill or dies. Transition in the hospital setting is constant and events such as discoveries in bio-

medicine, new members of staff arriving, junior members of staff becoming more senior and perhaps seeking greater autonomy in their work may give rise to problems. It is interesting to note that these problems in hospitals are similar to those in families because they may present 'symptoms' or difficulties which indicate relationship problems. A child in a family who bed-wets or steals, may have become unsettled as a result of difficulties in the relationship between his parents. Similarly, absenteeism in a hospital department may stem from poor morale and ineffectual management.

5. Reciprocity prevails in the *consultation setting*. Consultation is not a process of 'doing-something-to-someone'. It is best defined as a dialogue between the consultant and the consultee and may include other colleagues. Feedback between all systems must constantly be evaluated and processed by all participating systems. Furthermore, all institutions operate in a wider political and economic system. If a hospital is, for example, unable to offer a particular specialized treatment, this will in turn influence the care of patients. Health care staff may then have to deal with the frustration and anger of patients who feel that they are not being offered the full range of possible treatments.

6. Hospitals are *organizations of great complexity*. It is to be expected that problems will arise between members of staff, between the staff and patients and between both staff and patients, and visitors, relatives and suppliers to the hospital, all of whom are linked to the institution in some way. It is impossible to have consensus about everything. Staff, patients and ideas in medical science are constantly changing.

7. Problems that present to consultants are generally *expressed in language* and in the course of a conversation. Consultation is mostly a conversation about a problem. Family-Systems theory has contributed significantly to insights about language, problems and solutions.

Defining the Problem

Problems may relate to many different pressures such as staff relationships, patient management, confusion over tasks, the introduction of new protocols, and so on. Problems prompt people to think and to talk, and for this reason, a problem is a signal that brings into focus relationship issues. The first task of the consultant is to get a clear description of the 'problem'. The consultant *should not presume either* the presence or the nature of the problem until defined by the consultee or by others within the hospital with whom they relate.

The first problem-defining tasks for the consultant are to:

> a. elicit a description of the problem

> b. identify for whom the problem is a problem, and

> c. respond to changing views of the problems over time.

During the course of consultation it may emerge that other people are affected by the problem and they may need to be included in session. Some examples of different contexts of problems are listed below. These are taken from our AIDS counselling work.

Examples from AIDS Counselling

> **1.** *The problem presented concerns the relationship between the AIDS specialist and members of the AIDS counselling unit.* Example: The AIDS specialist asks members of the AIDS counselling unit to spend more time in his increasingly busy clinics. This leaves the counsellors with less time for working with other specialists.

> **2.** *The problem presented is related to people outside the hospital who come into contact with the unit.* Example: The volunteer 'buddy' system has changed its geographical boundaries which means that there are now fewer volunteers for the local catchment area. This will result in more work for hospital-based professionals.

> **3.** The problem presented is related to other support staff

who are required to liaise with the AIDS unit. Example: The health advisor in a sexually transmitted diseases clinic thinks that a patient, who is HIV antibody positive, should continue to be seen in that clinic as 'having an AIDS case on the books' is good for his promotion, but he does liaise with or discuss the case with the AIDS counsellors.

4. The problem presented is related to the team within which the counsellor works. Example: In order to cover all the outpatient clinics, it is not possible for the whole counselling team to ever meet all together. This has implications for internal communication, feelings of belonging-ness and morale within the unit.

The consultee is but one part of the system with which the consultant works. Invariably there are other systems, for example managers, colleagues and patients which the consultant must also consider. Each of these people may have a different view of the problem. The immediate task of the consultant is to obtain a definition of the problem and to try to identify for whom this is a problem (for example, "What do you see as the main problem?" - "What do you think is your colleagues view?"- "What made you decide to discuss this today?") It may be that soliciting different views of the problem constitutes the initial consultation focus. The definition of the problem, as it is seen by others, helps the consultant to begin to construct a new map or idea about the problem. The consultant is interested in how and why something is being explained in a particular way as this helps to further clarify and define the problem. It is then important to move to a higher level and to try to understand how and why *we* as consultants have understood something in particular way (for example, "What was it that John said that gave you the impression that there is rivalry between the nurse managers?"). Problem formulation is therefore a continuous and on going process. We are not trying to discover some truth; instead we are trying to define what is a problem and for the consultee, and why. Over time, ideas are revised and this may lead to the resolution of the problems or a different view of the same problem. Both problems and solutions may have a ripple effect in the hospital. The consultant can help to address this by drawing the attention of the consultee to the dilemmas (advantages and disadvantages) inherent in problems. This also helps to preserve a sense of neutrality. Thus, a consultant might say to the consultee:

"What new problems do you think would emerge in the radiotherapy department if specialist nurses were employed to help with the caseload?"

Planning the Consultation

A number of steps may be followed in planning any consultation. These are not necessarily rigidly applied. A colleague who asks for five minutes of time to discuss a case does not necessarily expect to be taken through each stage. The structure offers some guidance in the consultation procedure and it is especially useful where there is apparent 'stuckness' or difficulties in the consultation. The consultant may have overlooked some steps or procedures and this may have lead to confusion about the consultation task. The stages are listed below.

Stages of Consultation

1. Understanding the request for consultation and defining the problem.
2. Developing ideas about the consultant-consultee relationship.
3. Discussing a consultation contract.
4. Conversations about the problem.
5. Feedback and re-evaluating the contract.
6. More conversations about the problem.
7. Feedback
8. Ending the contract. Discussion about follow-up.
9. Re-assessing the consultant-consultee relationship.
10. Case closure

The first stage of understanding the request for consultation has already been described in this chapter. Some of the next stages are described in more detail below.

Understanding the Consultant-Consultee Relationship

It is the *relationship between the consultant and consultee* that most highlights the difference between internal consultation and external consultation. There are some advantages to the consultation situation between colleagues in the same department or hospital. They may for example be shorter in duration, take place at short notice and the consultee may benefit from the special expertise of a colleague in a particular field of health care. On the other hand, there is the danger that the consultant may be less neutral to the problem. We have drawn up a list of questions to ourselves to help us clarify our thoughts about the consultant-consultee relationship:

* Is there consensus in the consultee's department that the consultation should be requested?

* Is there an expectation that the consultation will uphold a particular view (i.e. he will not feel that he can introduce new or potentially controversial ideas)?

* Hierarchically, does the consultant have some autonomy and flexibility in relation to the consultee?

* From the point of view of their professional backgrounds, is there likely to be some measure of fit between the consultant and consultee?

A further step is for us to attempt to understand as much as possible about what effect it might have on their relationship if the consultation goes ahead. It is important to understand whether the consultee is trying to create an alliance with the consultant (bring him closer); hand over work or a task to him (redefine it as a liaison relationship); or perhaps discredit him by sabotaging the consultation (push him away). A useful way to speculate about these processes is to ask questions of oneself:

* What *relationship* do I already have with the *consultee* that may affect the nature, course and outcome of consultation?

* Should I choose *not to participate* or accept the consultation request, what might happen with regard to the *problem* and with regard to my *relationship* with the consultee?

* What *other parts of the organisation* might be affected by my participation, and how might they view my involvement in this problem?

* Are there any *particular 'cultural' or organisational rules* which would impede in work, e.g. as a consultant am I at liberty to bring

into the conversation anything about the doctor-patient relationship with the doctor?

* If the *problem were to deteriorate*, how would I relate to the consultee?

* Given that this consultation is offered on the basis of 'goodwill' and is not being paid for, how will this affect our *contract* and *respective obligations*?

* What *levels of the hospital system* (e.g. Senior Manager) might need to be involved and how might this *affect my position in the institution* if I had to engage them in our consultation?

* Should I become *'stuck'* in the course of the consultation, *with whom can I consult* without breaching *confidentiality* relating to my work with the consultee?

* How will I deal with *confidential information* relating to the case that may be important for the *process and outcome* of the consultation?

* To whom am I *ultimately contracted* and does this person have the *authority to enter* into consultation and *institute any changes*?

Before proceeding with the consultation, it is helpful to discuss some of the points with the consultee.

Discussion with the Consultee

Once some ideas have been developed about the relationship with the consultee a meeting can be arranged to discuss any of the points listed above which might impede in the consultation process. Prompt attention to a consultation request in a hospital setting is vital given that in the most extreme cases, the request may relate to life and death issues. In addition, circumstances change rapidly and prompt discussion may help to resolve problems that could exacerbate if they are left for any length of time.

Internal consultants, as opposed to external consultants, are in a unique position to respond quickly to problems in hospital. A meeting is arranged with the person who requests the consultation in the first instance. Some meaning has to be given to the meeting and for this reason one might define the purpose of the meeting as follows:

Consultant: Dr Smith, thank you for coming up to my office this morning. I think we agreed to meet for ten minutes and to arrange for another meeting if we need some more time. As you may recall, I said to you over the 'phone that before I could undertake consultation meetings with you and members of your department, I would first like to think over some ideas about my working with you over this problem. The reason for this is that in my experience, the success of consultation depends on several things. These include being clear about my role, my task and my relationship with you now and in the future. I think that it is especially important to think these over because we need to consider whether I am the most suitable person to be working with you and also because I want to feel that our relationship can withstand some pressure if things did not turn out in the way you had anticipated. Firstly, do you have any thoughts about this?

Consultee: Well actually I'm very pleased you've brought this up. It was not an easy decision for me to approach you, particularly because I know you're very busy and also because, frankly, Dr Jones (the co-director) had some thoughts that maybe we should be approaching someone outside of the hospital.

Consultant: How did it come about that you asked me?

Consultee: Dr Jones and I had heard about your work in the Rheumatology Unit and in fact it was he who first suggested we get in touch with you. I think he got cold feet, though, when he thought that if things 'went wrong', so to speak, that it would make it difficult to refer patients to your counselling team in the future. I suppose he was trying to protect our very good working relationship.

Consultant: If there were any disagreement or problems in our relationship, how might you handle the situation?

Consultee: I know that I could always talk to you. Perhaps Dr Jones would be more inclined to blame me and also remind me that we might have been better off with someone outside.

Consultant: How has it come about that he has chosen not to come to this meeting? (and so on).

Consultant: How do people in your own department react to this?

Consultee: I think some are having second thoughts about having taken me on in the first place.

Discussing a Contract

Making a contract is a part of the consultation process. It is the basis of an agreement between the consultee and the consultant as to what will be discussed in the course of consultation, how long it may take to work on the problem and to clarify professional boundaries. A contract engenders agreement to consult over a piece of work. This may be implicit in some work relationships such as between colleagues. It is important to establish whether the consultee has the authority to enter into a contract. The consultee might be asked:

> "To whom do you report? Is he aware of our meetings? Do you need his permission in order to be discussing these problems with us? How might it affect things with him if you were to set aside two hours a week in clinic time to meet with us?"

Some provision must be made for flexibility within this. For this reason, the contract does not set out conditions or fixed end points, but rather guides the consultant-consultee in their relationship until the contract is re-negotiated by virtue of new and evolving problems or ideas. The contract might take some of the following points into account:

1. There is an agreement to meet for consultation.

2. There is an agreement to participate in and contribute to the meetings.

3. The consultant can ask for something from the consultee.

4. The consultant may work with a team of colleagues.

5. What is said in the context of consultation is confidential to the

consultation context.

6. Each person takes responsibility for what they say.

7. Consultation is to be distinguished from any other collaborative clinical work between the teams or any members of the teams.

8. Meetings will take place at a specific time in a specified place for a specified length of time.

9. Certain people will be expected at meetings. Procedures are agreed in the event of any one of them not being able to attend or if someone has to leave the meeting.

10.   Financial arrangements pertaining to the consultation are agreed.

(**Note:** The internal consultant rarely charges for his work. For this reason, there should be some discussion about this with the consultee. It is helpful to state that under other conditions, consultation is usually charged for, but because this is among colleagues, there is no charge. On the other hand, impartiality may be jeopardised if any other conditions or favours are linked to consultation. It is, for example, not acceptable to agree to offer consultation in exchange for use of clinic space or staff.)

Once the contract is agreed on in more formal consultation situations, the consultation can proceed. However, in a hospital setting, not all problems that are discussed between colleagues are formally negotiated or take place in a designated place, at a pre—arranged time. Most consultations take place at the nurses station, in ward meetings, in the staff canteen, in corridors or over the telephone. It helps to keep a contract in mind even if there is no formal agreement or definition that consultation is taking place. An approach by someone for help with ideas for writing a letter to a colleague is an example of this.
 Sometimes we are asked if we have a rule about whether to consult in one's office or in the consultees own work setting. *Where* consultation takes place is important as this may influence the process. It might seem more formal if the consultee comes to the consultant's office, for example. On the other hand, the consultee may be unable to leave the ward and on-site consultation may have

to be arranged. We then go through a ritual of taking some charge of the space by arranging the seating and talking about time boundaries. Agreements have to be made about what will happen if there is a telephone call or if a member of staff is 'bleeped'.

The initial stages of internal consultation have been described in this chapter. These stages amount to a 'map' which conveys a procedure for setting-up and organising consultation sessions. More ideas about the tasks of the internal consultant, conducting the sessions and interviewing techniques are set out in the next chapter.

THE PROCESS OF INTERNAL CONSULTATION

PART II:

CONDUCTING THE CONSULTATION

The process of internal consultation is inextricably linked to the task of the consultant. In this chapter we describe both the consultant's task as well as the skills and procedures which can be used in order to carry out this task.

The Task of the Consultant

Consultation can help to define, clarify and solve problems through a conversation between the consultee and consultant. The *task* of the consultant is:

> *Through a conversation, to help the consultee to define and clarify problems, and find his own solutions by increasing the competence of the consultee and the options or choices available to him without blaming anyone or invalidating a particular view.*

The consultant helps to create an environment in which change can occur. While change may be sought, the consultant may not have any control over the direction of change or decisions made by the consultee.

Consultants in hospital settings might consider whether it is a prerequisite for them to have a comprehensive understanding of the medical condition with which the consultee works. Certainly some basic knowledge can help in the initial problem-defining phase. In haemophilia care, for example, one might guess that being a life-long and chronic condition, problems may manifest between staff and patients as the latter have to attend regularly for their care over many years and close staff-patient relationships may develop. Questioning is particularly helpful for gathering information and exploring initial ideas. Examples of questions to a consultee in relation to general medical problems are listed below:

How has it come about that there has been a shift in emphasis from inpatient to outpatient care?

What was happening at around the time when this was upgraded from a unit to a department?

Can you tell us something about community care arrangements?

If a patient were to become ill out of hours, what arrangements have you made for staff cover?

What are the particular aspects about working with this group of patients that might be different or stressful?

How is the handover organised to the new staff?

What do you think is unique to your work with this group of patients which sets your needs apart from other units in the hospital?

Who outside of this unit most recognise this?

In the absence of a comprehensive understanding of particular medical conditions, the consultant can work effectively by asking questions, and by drawing on examples from other medical problems. It takes many years of training and experience to become an accomplished therapist. The same is probably true of reaching the stage of being used as a consultant. Most consultants already have many years of experience and hold positions of some seniority, be they managerial or clinical. A few skills for conducting the consultation are described below.

Formulating Hypotheses

It helps to make an hypothesis or calculated guess about problems before the first and each subsequent consultation session. The hypothesis is based on available information (e.g. who requested the consultation, with what in mind) and helps to focus the questioning for each consultation interview. 'Hypothesizing' in this sense does not suggest 'proof' in the scientific empirical sense. Rather, it is a procedure which can help the consultant to organise his thinking and plan his interventions. Formulating an idea about what provoked the request for consultation and some ideas about the problems help to prepare the consultation before starting the session.

Any hypothesis should include the consultants ideas about the behaviour, beliefs and relationships relevant to the case. It is easy, and sometimes compelling to make a 'one-sided' hypothesis, that is, a linear hypothesis. A consultant may believe, for example, that a trainee in a psychology department fails to present case reports on the clients he is seeing because he cannot organize his time properly.

Through the use of circular questions (see below), the consultant may later understand that this is because the atmosphere of supervision is intimidating to the trainee. The supervisor in this case decided to bring the members of the department together for consultation. Support and consultation for the senior members of the psychology department staff as a regular activity had been overlooked. Consultation helped to address the problem of supervision and the idea of staff support in that department. The hypothesis needs to highlight not only the apparent problems, but also some of the dilemmas associated with the problems and its management, including some benefits accrued from having a problem.

Hypothesis can be formulated as soon as a request for consultation is made. Descriptions of the problem, as well as gaps in the story, are pieces of information that can be drawn on by the consultant. The hypothesis evolves as more information becomes available and as the consultation proceeds. A useful idea to apply when putting together ideas for an hypothesis is to reflect on how and why the consultants have come to understand the problem in a particular way. We ask the question: 'What has been happening to influence our own thinking in this particular way?' Hypothesizing can be of strategic value to the consultant as the process helps to create some distance between the consultant and the consultee. This in turn helps the consultee reduce his bias towards any one person or idea as the consultee, his context and all those connected with the problem have to be taken into consideration.

Some initial questions to the consultee about the hypothesis in a first session may include the following:

What has prompted you to be in contact with us?

Why now? What would you most like to see changed?

What would you most want to keep as it is?

When did the idea of consultation first come about?

What are your ideas of consultation?

What is happening in and around the unit?

Who first spoke about this problem in the unit?

Have new staff recently joined the unit? Has someone recently left?

What will inform us that the case can be closed and that we no longer need to be discussing this problem?

Formulating and Using Circular Questions

When a problem is described, the consultant can ask questions in order to elicit more views and to clarify ideas. There are some advantages to asking questions. Firstly, they help to introduce new ideas and new connections. Secondly, they are less confronting than statements. Thirdly, they create an atmosphere of interest and enquiry. Fourthly, they help to keep people involved in the discussion, be encouraging interest in the views that the consultant is attempting to elicit. Fifthly, circular questions address relationships and beliefs (see Campbell, Draper and Huffington, 1989). Sixthly, by asking questions, the consultant has some control over the focus and direction of the discussion. Answers to questions provide feedback and are invitations to more questions. However, just hearing the questions can help to introduce new views. Consultants may create some balance between the number of questions they ask and the number of statements they make. Questions can be of several kinds:

Type of Question	Example
Closed-ended (linear)	Can you keep your appointment?
Open-ended	What gives you evidence for that?
Hypothetical	If she doesn't resign today how will you continue with the research?
Future-oriented	If these problems with the laboratory continue, at what stage would you consider using a laboratory in another hospital?
Difference	Is it more or less stressful to give the results to patients without a nurse present?
Relationship	If your colleagues had heard you say that, how might it affect your relationship with them in the future?

Other interviewing techniques

Hypotheses and questions are used to guide the consultant, and in turn to assist the consultant to solve his problem. In addition, the consultant may apply other skills which help the consultee to view his problem in a different light, and hopefully, thereby develop new ideas about how to solve the problem. Four skills can be used in conversations which can help to introduce new ideas about a problem:

Validation:	respecting all the views and not aligning oneself with any particular view through questioning
Amplification:	taking one idea and examining many problems, solutions and ideas associated with it, by asking 'difference' and 'relationship' questions
Simplification:	reducing overly complex ideas to more simple and manageable problems by ranking concerns
Reframing:	introducing a new idea about a problem usually by suggesting what might have been gained by having the problem.

Linking ideas with behaviour, relationships and beliefs

Throughout the course of the sessions the consultant may wonder: 'Where do I go to from here?' Sometimes it is not immediately clear which lead should be followed or what should be said next. The interview process is made easier if the consultant tries to establish links between ideas or statements, behaviour, relationships and beliefs. The following diagram (page 33) illustrates how this can be done.

'Dreaded' issues

In our consultation work we identify and talk about 'dreaded issues', or what people fear the most about their having a problem. The fear may be in relation to the consequences of the problem not being solved. Similarly, in a consultation there may be issues or outcomes that are 'dreaded' by the consultee. These may include a fear of dismissal, being ignored in decision making, or not being put forward for promotion. Hypothetical and future-oriented questions are an effective way to address these fears ahead of time.

The following examples of such questions might be used in order to help the consultee to discuss his fears:

A. INFORMATION/STATEMENTS
Consultee: "I don't seem to get along
with colleagues in the Haematology

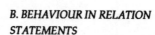

**D. BELIEFS ABOUT
STATEMENTS**
Consultant: "Where do you get
the belief that others get along
better without you ?"

**B. BEHAVIOUR IN RELATION
STATEMENTS**
Consultant:"How does that show?"
Consultee:" They don't refer patients
to me anymore."

C. EFFECTS ON OTHERS (Relationships)
Consultant: "How do people in your own department
react to this?"
Consultee: "I think some are having second thoughts
about having taken me on in the first place."

Techniques to help Define and Resolve Problems

Who is ultimately responsible for this case?

What implications would there be if the patient were to die
/ commit suicide?

What would be the worst possible thing that you could
imagine happening in this case?

What, in your view, is the difference between secrets and
confidentiality?

What recent changes in staff have there been and what
changes do you anticipate?

What would happen if the unit was forced to close?

Where does your support come from?
What do you see as your task and that of the unit?

What has to happen in order for you to feel that

you have done the best you can?

If this problem persists, how do you see things for
yourself in relation to this unit?

Being a part of the system

The internal consultant is a part of a wider hospital system.
Inevitably, there will be situations in which the consultant considers
he is 'stuck' or unable to move the consultation on in any direction.
An ability to recognise that one's own position may exacerbate an
impasse is essential for the internal consultant. It may be, for
example, that confidential information discussed in the course of
the consultation impedes in the clinical work of the consultant.
Seeking consultation from others, either within or outside of the
hospital is a significant step towards resolving this impasse.

Ending the consultation and arranging follow-up

The consulting team will usually meet to discuss their ideas about
the consultation session immediately after the session has ended.
This allows the group to examine the questioning and feedback in
the light of the discussion. Revisions may be made to the initial
hypothesis and the contract reviewed. The latter would be discussed
with the consultee at the start of the next session. In the post-session
discussion one might specifically address what beliefs had emerged,
what had changed and what remained the same, what effect the
consultation might have on the wider system and what effect it
might have on our relationship with the consultee outside of the
consultation context. The process of hypothesizing, consulting,
reviewing the feedback and contract continues until there is
agreement that the initial (or revised) goals of consultation have
been reached, or there is agreement, for whatever other reason, to
end the consultation. At the end of consultation, the consultant and
consultee need to discuss:

How they will work together in the future.

What follow-up is to be arranged (if any).

What changes there might be in their relationship.

What will remain unchanged.

What procedure will be followed if the problem recurs.

What feedback (if any) about the consultation needs to be presented to a third party.

This process provides an important opportunity for the consultant to avoid being redrafted in to carry out more work, even after the contract has ended, and for the re-creation of the appropriate boundaries between colleagues.

Summary

The consultation process should be guided by a structure or map. This reflects the consultants view of problems and how he might deal with them. The map need not be rigidly applied, but it does serve to keep a focus on the task, the goals and the processes associated with implementing and achieving these. In the rest of the book, a series of consultation examples are described in order to illustrate some of the points made in this and the previous chapters. The examples incorporate comments about theoretical issues, practical problems, and different approaches to problems. Extracts of dialogue are included in order to provide a sense of the consultation process. Different situations are described in order to illustrate the diverse range of problems which may prompt a request for consultation in the hospital setting.

CONSULTATION TO A COLLEAGUE ABOUT MANAGING STAFF/CLINICAL PROBLEMS:

CONSULTATION IN ACTION

Probably the most common situation for internal consultation is a case discussion between colleagues. Through discussion, the consultee attempts a different solution of the problem, without the case being taken over by the consultant, as would appear with a referral. Difficulties over the management of clinical cases are common in hospitals because multi-disciplinary team work does not automatically imply consensus over how best to manage a case. Hospital (and professionals) have rules and guide-lines for problem solving, although these are constantly being tested by developments in biomedicine, medical ethics, management practice and professional practice. Small crises such as an unexpected patient death, change of staff, staff handover, media publicity, strikes and so on may give rise to new difficulties which require problem solving. These may present as interpersonal or interprofessional conflicts. It should be stressed that problems of this kind are a normal and expected occurrence in hospital.

In the example set out below a social worker asked a counsellor colleague to consult him over the management of an unexpected patient death. Through the consultation it became apparent that the anxiety aroused by the case highlighted a staffing problem with the nurses. Discussion about the case between the consultant and consultee helped to clarify the problem and the options for solving it. The following consultation tasks can be identified:

Defining and clarifying the problem

Identifying who else is involved or affected

Mapping out the professional hierarchy which is involved

Identifying whose problem it is and how the consultee might respond to it

Considering the choices or options available to the consultee, and the implications of any of these

Reviewing whether similar problems have presented in other clinical work

Arranging for follow up or feedback

Note: *that the consultant makes no assumptions and asks many questions rather than prescribing solutions. These questions mostly concern ideas, beliefs, choices, future implications of decisions and professional relationships.*

Social Worker: I'd like to ask you advice about a problem that I faced over the weekend at 7.00 in the evening.

Counsellor: You mean you were called out on the bleep?

Social Worker: Yes, I was called into the hospital. The house physician called me on the advice of the doctor in charge of this patient. The house physician said that the patient had unexpectedly arrested and died, and that she wanted me to come in and help to tell the relatives.

The social worker describes the event that led to a request for consultation. Now the counsellor as consultant gathers more specific information about the event.

Counsellor: I know from our own work that we do this from time to time, but it is always helpful to consider why you think this particular team at this particular point asked you to come and help.

Social Worker: I think the reason for calling me in was that there was some panic about the unexpected death. It may also have to do with the special funding for more specialist nurses and I feel that there is still a shortage of these specialist nurses on the ward.

Counsellor: Just so that I understand, do these specialist nurses have any remit for working with the family of the patient?

Social Worker: They should and they would be willing to if they had the time.

Counsellor: So who in the medical and clinical team do you think was most concerned about the case?

> *Now the consultant tries to identify: for whom is the problem a problem?*

Social Worker: I think both the doctor and nurse. But for me, the problem was a different one. I had to spend time with a very hysterical sister of the patient who didn't really expect this death either. Also, there was a suspicion at the time that the patient had killed himself.

Counsellor: What did you say to the nurses after you had seen this hysterical sister?

Social Worker: I really didn't give much feedback, other than to say that one of the problems was that of time and under-staffing. The sister on the ward had the special leukaemic patients to deal with and there were two more who were terminal and dying. The ward also had one other patient had just returned from ITU (intensive care).

Counsellor: Which of the nursing staff, if any, would also have agreed with you that they were short-staffed and unable to offer the care that they usually would?

> *The problem of under-staffing now emerges and the consultant now explores some implications of this in*

*terms of how it affects people's work and whether there
have been any attempts to deal with staffing difficulties.*

Social Worker: That's an important question you put to me because
at the time I think that, although the ward sister would have been
aware of it, she was so busy with her jobs and splitting herself in two
that I don't think she was as clear all along as I was.

Counsellor: Do you think that she had previously discussed
these staffing problems on the ward with anyone in her own
management hierarchy?

Social Worker: One of the problems that I wanted to bring to you
is that I am not sure how forceful she is in putting forward her
stresses to her own hierarchy.

Counsellor: What evidence do you have for that? Also, what do
you feel is the main problem: the understaffing or the ward sister's
difficulty in approaching her own hierarchy?

> *The consultant seeks clarification of the statement and
> evidence of behaviour which supports a particular
> belief.*

Social Worker: The problem continues and here I saw it again, and
you and I know that it has been there before.

Counsellor: Has she or any of her senior colleagues tried to
approach anyone in the nursing hierarchy at all?

Social Worker: I'm not sure and that's why I feel it is important at
this point, that you and I consider the next best step.

Counsellor: So what did you have in mind to do now that you have
some experience of quite a difficult case here?

Social Worker: What I have done is to get the whole thing off my
chest in a letter to the senior nursing manager. So now the question
is, what about this letter of mine?

Counsellor: What special message do you think you are giving to
the nurse managers when it comes from you? And how might that

be different if it came from the nurses and doctors?

> *The consultant now suggests that the social workers*
> *attempted solution of writing a letter may create a new*
> *problem. Note that the consultant does not oppose the*
> *consultees idea but asks questions about the implications*
> *of the letter.*

Social Worker: I suppose in writing the letter my idea was twofold. One, to put down the events as I saw them on that evening, and then to provide some concrete examples of where I actually witnessed a staff shortage. But my hesitation is just what you are raising now that maybe coming from me, it will impede rather than help in what we are trying to achieve.

Counsellor: Could you say a bit more about that?

Social Worker: It may mess things up because it is us, the social workers asking for more of something again. You have begun to make me even more aware that the problem seems to lie with this particular sister on the ward who has been found to be under great stress recently and we are not sure whether she has 'communicated' enough of that stress to her immediate superiors, never mind the higher nursing hierarchy.

Counsellor: I am not saying don't send the letter, but let's just think how one can help the senior nursing sister on the ward to communicate more effectively with her own hierarchy if that is what is needed. Do you have any ideas?

Social Worker: The first thing perhaps is to go back to her now and find out from her and the staff nurse what for them do they see to be the major stresses. Maybe their stresses were not the same as mine.

Counsellor: Perhaps. Who else would you include in that meeting? Would you include the doctors or would you keep it just with the nurses at this stage?

> *The consultant helps the social worker to respond to the*
> *problem in a practical way by asking for specific ideas*
> *about how he wants to go about solving the problem.*

Social Worker: I think at the first stage, I would like to include the doctor who was on duty that evening. I know from reports from the sister who I telephoned the following day, that both of them were extremely upset after the incident.

Counsellor: There are two things here that I would like us to think about. The first is how, and should you help the nursing sisters in their tasks? Also, what would be the implication of our being involved in this case and pushing it through and up the nursing hierarchy, and how would that reflect on our unit and our clinical work in the hospital?

> *An essential issue is to highlight the potential problems it may raise for the consultee to attempt to solve the problem.*

Social Worker: I think it would possibly be taken as going beyond my remit.

Counsellor: What implications does that have for our unit?

Social Worker: I think when we are seen to go beyond our remit, the result is a tendency to cut us out of decision making.

Counsellor: Is there any particular idea that stands out from our discussion?

> *The consultant offers the consultee an opportunity to comment on the consultation process before drawing it to a close.*

Social Worker: I had to write the letter, but really, it's not a good idea for me to send it. That in itself could go against what we are trying to achieve.

Counsellor: Do we need to meet again to review this particular case?

Social Worker: I think what would be interesting is to meet again with the nurse and doctor to see if things have changed at all, perhaps in a few weeks from now.

This consultation lasted ten minutes. The consultee was helped to consider the implications of his taking over some of the remit of a senior nurse which might have otherwise created new problems for the consultee. The consultee was helped to put some of the responsibility for problem solving back to the nurses which might reduce the consultee's stress. The solution of not directly approaching the nurse managers might be slower, but in the long term it may prove more viable and impactful. The consultation provided an opportunity for thinking before acting. This clinical problem also allowed the consultant and consultee to reflect on their relationships with colleagues. It is difficult to empirically assess whether the consultee made a good or bad decision, although he had clarified for himself the implications of how he intended to act.

CONSULTATION TO A CLINICAL SUPERVISOR

CONSULTATION IN ACTION

Supervision should not be confused with consultation. In the context of supervision, the supervisor has a responsibility for the clinical work and the professional practice of the supervisee. In consultation, the consultant has no clinical responsibility for the case; this remains with the consultee. Consultation about supervision is a further context for problem-solving in the hospital setting.

In this example, a case is described in which a social worker is consulted by a nurse supervisor responsible for running a staff group in a renal unit. She asked a social worker for help with running the group. The nurse supervisor claimed that she was having difficulty in supervising the work of one of the group as the latter seemed to ignore any of her advice. The social worker first agreed to consult to the supervisor about the group but did not undertake to attend or participate in the group. The social worker explained that her joining the group may make the situation worse as it could undermine the authority of the supervisor in the group and heighten the tension between the group member and supervisor. It could also give the impression that the social worker and supervisor were in an alliance against this particular person. The supervisor and social worker agreed to meet in the social work department for half an hour to discuss the problem. The social worker, acting as a consultant, thought about covering the following points in the first meeting:

Define the problem

Identify how the problem presents itself to the consultee and how it has been dealt with thus far

Consider options for alternate solutions

Help the consultee to find practical ways of improving her supervisory skills without undermining her competence

Discuss whether follow-up is needed and how this should be offered.

Supervisor: As you know, I've been running a supervision group for the nursing staff who work with renal patients in in-and out-patient settings. We have been meeting for six months. One of the problems that I have recently had is with a community nurse one member who comes to the group. She has attended regularly, and at our last session it was her turn to present a case. I had difficulty in supervising her case because I found that in many ways her work was not structured. I had a particular problem when she started telling me she had spent seven hours with a patient at home holding his hand and talking to him. I had a concern not only about the other clinical work which she is doing, but felt that perhaps she is unable to assign priorities and doesn't know when to pass on her cases, or when to get advice from other professional staff.

Social Worker: What were the steps that you took to try and point out to her perhaps your views about this might differ from hers, and there might be a different way of handling this patient?

The consultant immediately addresses the supervisory relationship but does not take sides with either the nurse supervisor or the community nurse.

Supervisor: I'm afraid, I think that when I started out with her I was perhaps a bit sarcastic and asked her how she managed to get through a full days' work, if she spent seven hours with just one patient. She said that she thought that the professional task here was to make sure that all of the patients felt secure and supported, and she would never leave anyone who was depressed. I then asked her if there was anyone else with whom she works, who could help her in that task. She said 'no'. She's on her own in the community.

Social Worker: That's just given me an idea. In the same way that you asked her if she had anyone else to help her with that patient, was there anyone else in the group who could help you achieve your task, perhaps, more easily than you did?

> *The consultant is at liberty to offer possible solutions,*
> *but this is done in a non-prescriptive way, that is in the*
> *style of ...'have you thought of' rather than 'do this'.*

Supervisor: There might have been, but I don't know enough about her particular work. There's a nurse from Accident and Emergency and staff there are used to dealing with acute situations where they have time pressures and where they have many other patients in the waiting room. I saw her roll her eyes back when she heard her colleague talk about her particular work. But I wasn't sure how to engage her or how to use her.

Social Worker: What might you do to engage someone?

Supervisor: I felt a lot of the pressure was on me. Perhaps I could have put it back to other members of team and ask each person their view about how they saw this case.

Social Worker: Yes, that's exactly what I mean, because in some ways what happened at the beginning of the session as you report it, reflects very much what's happening with the liaison nurse and her patient. So you and the nurse were into a dialogue and you were taking on all the responsibilities. If you carried on as you would with a patient being seen in the context of his family, maybe some of the responsibility would have been taken off you because the others might well feed back other ideas.

> *Without blaming the supervisor, the consultant points*
> *out how she can use the group to solve the problem and*
> *thereby potentially avoid a direct confrontation between*

the supervisor and the nurse.

Supervisor: That makes a lot of sense. I think when we first started this group, we had an ideas that there were one or two members of the group who did not have support in their work outside the hospital. In a sense I see that she continues to work on her own and at another level she is asking for support from her colleagues. She was one of the staff who said that we should be appointing a second community nurse to work alongside her. So perhaps she is bringing this problem to the group, in order to reinforce and underline her need for support.

Social Worker: Which gets us back to the nursing hierarchy. As with similar problems we see in the hospital the task is to help her to be clearer about exactly what she wants and how she can best ask for that. Perhaps there also needs to be some more clarity about her task.

Supervisor: I think what I would like to do in the next session, is not only to ask her, but to ask each person in the group what they see as their actual task, and then to ask each other person in the group to comment on their view of what they think somebody's task should be. Maybe through that we will get some clarification, agreement and also maybe disagreement about what people should be doing, and that may lead to some new ideas.

> *The supervisor recognizes that the solution can, in this case, open the way for a potentially fruitful discussion about the task of the community nurse. This is evidence to the consultant that the consultee has not been de-skilled since she presents innovative ideas.*

Social Worker: That sounds very important because we always have to think about the purpose of these meetings, the tasks of the people we supervise, and our position and our role in the course of supervision.

> *The consultant generalizes about the problem and indicates that is a 'normal' problem that will probably recur.*

Supervisor: It also makes me think that the definition for this group was that it is a supervision group. It's not a consultation group and maybe I have to provide for a separate supervision meeting with a particular worker, where she can feel more supported in her work.

Social Worker: A thought occurs to me; it's a bit of a crazy idea. If you and I hadn't been able to have this conversation because say I was abroad, who else do you think you might have gone to about the problem, or how would you have dealt with it?

> *The phrase 'this may seem a crazy idea' is a particularly useful preface to any idea that may shock or be 'resisted', although, in this example, it is not used for this purpose. The consultant is trying to understand how the consultee goes about solving similar problems at work.*

Supervisor: I think I would have done one of two things. I would either have kept it to myself and thought about it, and perhaps come up with some solutions, although I don't think I would have had quite the same clarity that I have now. On the other hand, I may have taken it to the colleagues who work in your team downstairs, because I know that although they don't have experience with this particular group they have a lot of experience of working with teams and perhaps they would be able to offer some solutions.

Social Worker: One think I want to be quite clear about: when you say they are used to working with different teams, what exactly do you mean?

Supervisor: They don't have to work with the same clinical teams that I have to work with, but they also deal with colleagues who are doctors, nurses, counsellors, psychologists, and so on, and they also deal with in-and out-patients. I think the structures are the same, although the content and the specific problems will be very different, and for that I would want to draw on their experience.

The session ended after thirty minutes and the supervisor arranged to discuss any changes or problems with the social worker after the next supervision session. The supervisor agreed that the presence of the social worker in the group would possibly exacerbate the problem and for this reason the consultant was only with the consultee. If the consultant had been present at the meeting, the danger was that it could become supervision-of-supervision, which could undermine the nurse supervisor. In this example, the consultant is perhaps more prescriptive and interpretative than one might ordinarily be in the case. The consultant asks fewer questions than in the previous case. This is most likely to happen when there are constraints on time or where consultation lapses into supervision. This mode of consultation can be used to achieve a goal more rapidly. The consultant may want to offer 'good advice' based on experience, or may want to appear more credible and experienced. The preface 'In my experience of similar cases or problems...' can be reassuring for the consultee who feels uncertain about how the consultant will help with the problem. The essential difference between giving advice and supervison is that in the former, the consultee can choose as to whether advice will be taken up. Supervision is part of most working relationships in the hospital setting because of the hierarc hy of accountability. Consultation can help supervisors reflect on their task and the associated difficulties.

Changing from liaison to consultation in the course of clinical work

Consultation in action

Through experience we have learned that it is helpful if clinical work is preceeded by consultation, wherever possible. In some cases, consultation can obviate the neccessity for further clinical work. A new referral provides an oportunity for changing the emphasis from liaison to consultation work. In the example set out below, a ward sister telephoned our counselling unit in the hospital and asked for one of the counsellors to come up to the ward as soon as possible. She would not provide any further information over the telephone as she said it was dificult to speak from the nurses' station. It was a ward on which six months previously, there had been complications around counselling, testing and diagnosing a heterosexual man with HIV. In a case review, it was felt that if the counselling team had been involved in the case at an earlier stage, some of the management problems may not have been quite as serious. The first clue, therefore, from the new referral, was that there was considerable anxiety over the management of a similar case and that counsellors should be involved at a very early stage.

The counsellor who received the call briefed a colleague about the problem. They discussed the referral and drew up a list of questions they thought would guide the counsellor in his meeting with the clinical team. These included:

> Whose idea was it to make the referral?
>
> Was there agreement among team members to make the referral?
>
> Who else in the hierachy was affected?
>
> Were there any particular views about using an AIDS counsellor?
>
> How could we best help the team in their management of the patient?
>
> Was there any way in which members of the clinical team could be helped to undertake some of the counselling?

The ward sister introduced the counsellor to a senior registrar, house officer and two other nurses involved in the care of the patient. They met in the nurse's room where there was privacy. The meeting began by the nurse explaining why she was making the referral. In this case the counsellor is acting as the consultant.

Nurse: I have asked you to come up here today because we have a patient whom the doctors would like to test for HIV. As you remember, we had problems with the last case on this ward because we couldn't get the patient's consent and his wife was really very upset over the positive test result. I am very concerned that we don't repeat this.

Counsellor: Can you tell me whose idea it was that the counsellor should be called at this stage?

Nurse: It was my idea because this is a new medical team here and they weren't aware of the procedures involved and rules for getting a counsellor in when you want to test someone for HIV.

> *The nurse provides an explanation for why 'the problem' has recurred: the new arrival of a new medical team.*

Counsellor: Can I just check that everyone in the team here today feels the same way, that the patient needs to be tested?

Senior Registrar: There is no doubt about it. We have tested him for most other things and there are several symptoms that may indicate AIDS.

Counsellor: Is this also the view of the medical consultant in charge?

> *In the hospital setting medical consultant (specialists) have ultimate responsibility for patients and although the internal consultant may work with more junior staff on a day-to-day basis, his views and authority must be considered and respected.*

House Officer: Yes, we discussed it in our ward round today and he said that we should go ahead with testing. Just before we were going to take blood from him, the ward sister said that we have to call you to counsel him.

Counsellor: From the way that you've put it, it sounds that having a counsellor seems a complication for you that holds up the procedure.

Senior Registrar: Actually, it is the other tests that we are going to do with them, and I just want to get on and test him.

Counsellor: Yes, that's fine. I don't want to get in the way of any of your decisions. In what way could I help you in carrying out this task?

> *The consultant takes a non-oppositional stance. 'Setting oneself up as an expert' is an invitation for others to contest you at best, or sabotage your work, at worst. He does not tell people what they should do either.*

Senior Registrar: From what I hear, you have to talk to the patient to get his consent. Now I am a bit worried that if after talking to him he says 'no', then we are going to run into a bit of bother.

Counsellor: That gives me an idea. What I often do in similar cases is I talk to the medical and nursing teams beforehand and we the patient. You could then see the patient and do the counselling yourself. At any rate, I think it's probably better that you see him because you know him and my involvement may make him more anxious. Perhaps if you were to say to him that you are carrying out a series of tests, and one of them that you would like to carry out is an HIV test, that would help not draw any undue attention to this particular test.

House Officer: Actually, that's quite a relief to hear that, because we were discussing between ourselves over lunch, that this AIDS counselling business can be a hindrance.

Counsellor: I can see that you might consider talking routinely about blood tests as a hindrance. However, we do know from previous experience, as sister will tell you, that from time to time, you can run into difficulties, particularly with this test. In our last case, we were unable to obtain the consent of the patient, because he was neurologically impaired. His wife became very upset when she heard the result and we had many new problems to deal with.

> *The consultant stands his ground and draws on anecdote to support a particular idea.*

Ward Sister: It's a similar case to the one that we had the last time. The same problem of a married man presenting with symptoms similar to HIV and yet from the history that we obtained, no real risk.

Counsellor: So how would you introduce the topic of HIV testing with him ?

> *A practical step in managing the case is now discussed. The consultant draws on his experience in order to challenge ideas and introduce new ones.*

Senior Registrar: I would like to go in and say to him that so far we haven't been able to find anything from the tests that we've done, and that one of the tests we would now like to do is the HIV test.

Counsellor: If he says to you, "What is an HIV test", what are you going to say?
Senior Registrar: We can tell him that it's the test for the AIDS

antibodies and that we need his consent for this test.

Counsellor: Yes, that seems fine. It's also very important to obtain a detailed sex history from him. Has anyone done this yet?

House Officer: Yes, I've asked him a few question and he is happily married.

Counsellor: Have you asked him if he has had sexual partners outside of his marriage, or if he has ever injected drugs, or if he has ever received blood from a blood transfusion?

House Officer: Well, no. I didn't ask him that because he's married. I didn't think of it.

Counsellor: It is important, epidemiologically, to try to understand something about the risk. I would suggest that you specifically ask those questions. Often we find that by taking a detailed sex history, patients talk about a risk which they wouldn't ordinarily describe in the course of routine clerking.

> *Straightforward 'teaching' is not out of place in*
> *consultation as new information can lead to new ideas*
> *and ways of managing problems.*

Senior Registrar: But if the man is married then he's not homosexual.

Ward Sister: That's what others thought until we dealt with the last case. You can't tell about those things just by looking at somebody, and anyway he may have had sexual contacts with other women.

Counsellor: Is there any difficulty in asking him these personal questions ?

Senior Registrar: No, not really. I think you've given us some ideas now about the things that we can talk to him about. What happens though if he is positive?

Counsellor: That's a good question. Patients should be prepared for a positive test result. I think you would need to explain to him that there are specialists within the hospital who are available to deal with the problems that arise from having HIV infection. This important from an infection-control point of view to find out about this relationship with his wife. We need to know if he is still having a sexual relationship with her. If the patient turns out to be positive, and he is having intercourse with her, there is every reason to believe that she is at risk from him. Also, we need to know how old his daughter is. She might also be at risk from the mother if she is very young.

Senior Registrar: We'd never thought about that. Are you sure you don't want to come in and do the interview for us and you can feed back to us afterwards about what happened?

> *The consultant reinforces the competence of his colleagues where this is appropriate. Failure to have done so at this point would have meant that the case would have reverted to a referral.*

Counsellor: I would prefer not to because, as you said, you know the patient better than I do. Perhaps you can have your discussion with him and we can review it afterwards.

House Officer: That's fine. I'm quite prepared to take a chance with him and let's see how things go.

Counsellor: Alright. You know how to get hold of me. You've got my telephone and bleep numbers. Is there anything else that we need to discuss?

Senior Registrar: I just wanted to say that I'm less irritable now that I was when you were first called up here! It has been of some help and we will certainly get hold of you if there are problems and if he turns out to be positive.

This example illustrates how a referral can be used to consult with the referrer, identify and confront problems in the professional team and lead to consultation over a case. This may have the effect of improving how referrals are made in the future and even decreasing their numbers if some counselling skills are passed on. Consultation and liaison add variety to the scope of one's work. In this example, *the consultant attempts to strike a balance between adding complexity to the problem by teaching about it and describing or illustrating special skills, and helping their colleagues to feel sufficiently confident to undertake new work.* The consultant does not withdraw from the case at the end, but offers his assistance should it be needed. The consultant should describe how he can be used in relation to future cases as a way of maintaining his relationship with colleagues and conveying to them that he is not handing over all of his work and clinical remit. We have found that consultation work is often as time consuming as clinical work and the issues can be as, if not more complex.

Three different positions can be covered in moving from liaison to consultation, which are illustrated below. In the first position (A), the counsellor accepts the referral and sees the patient; in the second (B) a link is made with the referring person and together they see the patient; and in the last (C) the referrer keeps the case, undertakes the counselling and consults the counselling service over difficult cases.

Accepting the referral

Intermediary Counselling Structure

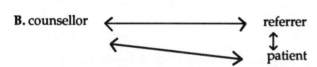

Consultation-Counselling Structure

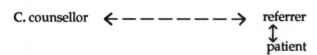

A difficulty arises when the referrer experiences problems and the consultant notes that the clinical work that remained with the consultee is not adequately carried out. It may be undermining to colleagues to revert back to a liaison structure. In these situations we suggest trying a few joint sessions and seeing the patient together with the colleague. We define this as a learning experience for us, but we hope to pass on some of our skills. Before the session we agree that one person will interview the patient and the other will observe and consult. If there are points which have not been addressed, the consultant will be free to point these out to his colleague during or towards the end of the session. In this way, the clinician retains control over the questioning and the session. This method of joint consultative sessions had proved helpful in general medical problem-solving, case management and in developing and enhancing relationships with colleagues.

SETTING UP AND DEVELOPING SERVICES IN THE HOSPITAL

CONSULTATION IN PRACTICE

Previous examples of consultation have highlighted some of the issues and dilemmas associated with clinical problems and their management. Consultation skills may also be applied to organisational transitions such as the setting-up and development of services in the hospital. The constant changes in staff, ideas, diagnostic and therapeutic approaches, policies and even physical structures in the hospital may give rise to problems which are seemingly of an administrative nature, yet they are inextricably linked to interpersonal processes. Foremost among these are questions about:

a. defining professional tasks

b. defining roles in the organisation

c. clarifying professional boundaries between colleagues and between patients and colleagues

d. clarifying professional accountability

e. developing inter-and intra-departmental professional relationships

f. evaluating services

Consultants may offer their expertise in relation to another department or unit in the hospital, or they may act as internal consultants to their own unit. The tasks of the consultant in relation the points listed above are problem-identification and problem-solving. The consultant may need to clarify: What will the consultation be about? With whom will the consultation be conducted? What will be the goal of consultation? and, How will it be carried out?

As an example we have chosen to illustrate this application of consultation by drawing on our experience of establishing a new AIDS counselling unit in our hospital. This was a planned consultation intervention which in some ways was successful and in other ways created, rather than solved problems. In retrospect, several discernible stages can be identified in our work. These are listed below:

Stages of Consultation over a New Clinical Service

1. Authorization for the project

2. Appointing the clinician-consultants

3. Soliciting ideas and views about the counselling task

4. Deciding with whom one should consult

5. Consultation

6. Feedback

7. Follow-up

1. Authorization for the project

It is unlikely that any project will come to fruition without the authority and support of hospital managers, in the first instance. They are responsible for budgets, policies and the tasks for most people in the organisation. It would therefore be a major error (if not contrary to operational policy) to initiate new projects, set up new teams or offer a new specialty without first discussing these with people in the managerial hierarchy. It is increasingly common to find clinically trained personnel in managerial positions. For this reason, any proposal for a new project is likely to be assessed not only for its merits, but also for the extent to which it overlaps with or detracts from other projects. The latter is more a secret agenda in hospital management teams. A psychologist on a management team may, for example, be alarmed at a proposal from social workers to extend their work into 'disaster counselling and support services', believing this to be the remit of his own specialty.

In our case, hospital managers were requested by the Department of Health in the UK to investigate the need for AIDS counselling. Thus the project had the authority of the managers from the outset. Setting up a new service within an existing organisation can present dilemmas. The first task may be to prepare oneself for challenges from colleagues such as "What experience do you have for doing that?, "Why do you seem to get more money and resources than us?" "What is the need for a new unit?" and so on. It is tempting to justify one's position to colleagues which can quickly lead to a symmetrical argument which leaves the novice consultant and colleagues feeling further apart. It is probably better to note any comments of this sort and to not offer long explanations for the work, in the initial stage. It seems that challenges to new ventures are an inevitable process in hospitals! In the present frugal climate in many hospitals, new services are usually viewed with envy by colleagues and arguments draw attention rather than deflect it. An initial task for the consultant is therefore to establish himself in his position without drawing too much attention to himself or his tasks. Additionally, he should seek a few allies in the hospital who will be supportive. The support of at least one person in authority (hospital manager or senior medical consultant) can help to ease the apparent isolation.

2. Appointing the consultants

Managers have to appoint the consultants for a new project and define their task. This in itself may be a situation for consultation. The consultants need to understand what exactly is expected of them in relation to the task, how this should be carried out, how it should be evaluated and what feedback is wanted. A time scale for setting up the service might also be negotiated. The consultants also need to be accountable to someone in management so that progress and problems can be monitored. Decisions will have to be made as to how the consultants, acting for the hospital managers, will be introduced to consultees in the hospital, in this case to colleagues. This may be in the form of an introductory letter, a telephone call or a personal visit.

3. Soliciting ideas and views about the consultation task

Some goals need to be set for the consultation exercise. In our case, we decided to conduct a series of consultations with a medical specialist. The purpose of these interviews was to provide us with an opportunity to consider how referrals could be made to the new service and how views about AIDS counselling and problems of patient management could be solicited. The primary goals that we listed were to:

a. Assess the specific needs of each specialist in relations to counselling.

b. Elicit some idea of how they viewed counselling and how this could fit into their work.

c. Gather some information about how referrals would be made.

d. Identify who else in each unit had experience working with AIDS/HIV infected patients and who had specific skills in relation to counselling and bereavement issues.

e. Outline how case notes would be kept and confidentially preserved.

f. Decide how feedback and evaluation of the counselling would be undertaken.

g. Identify and correct erroneous views about counselling.

These tasks guided us in our discussions with the medical specialists and helped us to keep a focus in these meetings.

4. Deciding with whom one should consult

Ideally, one would want to solicit the views of everyone in the hospital but practically this may not be possible. The decision to consult with certain staff requires careful planning. A general rule is to identify and consult with people in authority at the top of the medical, nursing, paramedical and administration hierarchies. Without their co-operation, any consultation or intervention at a lower level is likely to be thwarted. Those in higher authority have it as their task to 'give permission' (or to refuse) for the consultant to have access to more junior staff. Our first consultation phase engendered consulting with senior staff members only.

5. Consultation

The conversations with each specialist comprised many questions, examples of these are listed below:

Questions about the need for counselling
Can you think of a situation where you might need a counsellor?

Who else on your staff might agree with this? Who might disagree?

What is unique about the needs of patients under your care?

What would be important for us to know in relation to the AIDS/HIV infection problems you are faced with?

Questions to help explore the scope of counselling
What might you expect of a counsellor in relation to your patients?

How might counselling help you to manage your patients? In what way could it interfere with this?

Are there areas which you think counsellor should not touch on in work relating to these patients?
What do you think is the single most important contribution a counsellor could make to patients?

How might you deal with patients if there were no counselling service?

Which staff have appropriate experience?

Questions to help think about the referral process
When making the referral, what information do you think would be the most important for the counsellor to know?

At which point in time do you think a patient would need to see a counsellor?

What would convince you that a patient did not need counselling?

What clues do you think patients would give you to indicate they had a problem?

Questions about feedback and evaluation of sessions
How might you know if the patient were benefitting from counselling?

How can we deal with the issue of confidentiality in relation to giving you some feedback about the sessions?

What would you like us to feed back to you about the patient?

At what stage of the counselling would you want feedback?

What would you like us to achieve to conclude that we no longer have to counsel the patient?

Questions addressing the relationship between the counsellor and other members of staff on the ward
How would you see your staff in relation to the counsellor?

Who else on your staff counsels patients?

Who else on your staff is keen to work with these patients?

Who the least?

Who on your staff might be interested in sitting in on sessions with a counsellor?

Questions relating counselling to the wider hospital system

Do you see a place for staff counselling in relation to the AIDS/HIV infection problem?

Who on your staff might be able to take over from the counsellor?

At what point might others, such as the family be involved in counselling?

If the counsellor were to note that the patient were receiving conflicting messages from the staff, how might they deal with this?

The following is an extract from one such interview in which the counsellor as consultant, identifies whether a counsellor is needed and the implications of using a counsellor for the specialists own staff.

Counsellor: Can you think of a situation where you might need a counsellor?

Doctor: Maybe to discuss the antibody test with the patient.

Counsellor: What sort of issues do you think would be important to discuss?

Doctor: What it means and the implications ... and if it were positive.

Counsellor: If I were to summarise one such session with a patient, what would be most important for you to know?

Doctor: What they would do if they were positive and well, then I'd like to discuss with you what can be done for them.
Counsellor: Is there anyone else on your staff who might be in on such a discussion?

Doctor: Yes, the sister on the ward and my two registrars.

We found that many specialists were concerned that a counsellor might work in such a way that the social support and care was separated from the clinical care. This might arise where the counsellor did not feedback to the clinical teams or consult with them before a session. To prevent this we introduced the idea of a pre-sessions discussion with clinical staff. This helped to redefine 'counselling' as 'consultation' in some cases.

Counsellor: Dr Peterson, it seems that you would prefer to think about each case before referring the patient to me?

Doctor: Yes, perhaps the sort of patients we see in this unit are not able to really benefit from a chat with you; after all about 80% are unconscious or are being ventilated.

Counsellor: It might be helpful for me to know that you do have an AIDS/HIV infected patient under your care, just in case there are problems later with the family or in removing an infected body should the patient die.

Doctor: Oh yes? Actually two of the sisters on the ward have had to deal with the family before and I'm sure that they would want to help with that in future. Can they contact you?

Counsellor: Certainly. Since they already have experience in this it would be very interesting to meet with them and learn about how they dealt with the family.

Doctor: So could they sometimes talk to you about a patient?

Counsellor: Yes, I don't always have to meet with the patient.

The interviews with the medical consultant helped to provide some definition about what could be appropriate for referral to a counsellor. A relationship with the referrer was established and subsequent referrals provided feedback about this.

6. Feedback

Prior to initiating further consultation, the consultant needs to obtain feedback in order to plan the next series of consultation interviews. Different forms of feed-back might be relevant, including the extent and nature of clinical referrals, and responses of hospital managers to the viability of the project. One difficulty is that change in organisations is often slow and it may take many months, and in cases years, for any significant feedback. Furthermore, the observation of processes of which one is a part is problematic. Outside consultation can be helpful in this regard.

7. Follow-up

The next phase of the internal consultation should be inextricably linked to the feedback gathered from the first series of consultation. It may be that consultations with some senior members of staff have to be repeated before other people in the organisation are consulted. It is tempting to believe that changes are attributable to one's consultation interviews. From our experience, we have found that it was often events outside of our influence which also contributed to new views and ideas in the institution. The social climate regarding AIDS, HIV testing and care outside of the hospital proved impactful and compelling.

Conclusion

There are a number of lessons from using a consultative method for setting up a new service. Considerable energy needs to be invested in gaining the co-operation of management in any such major venture. Not only do they pay one's salary, but they also have to agree to the tasks their employees carry out. Regular meetings with members of the health authority and hospital management helped to keep them informed of problems and achievements, and to keep an appropriately high level of profile for the unit.

Meeting with those medical specialists at the top of the hierarchy helped in the same way. Had we first consulted to more junior members of staff, we might not have had any co-operation from medical personnel. This would have had implications for clinical management. Once we had secured their co-operation, we found we had much easier access to other members of their staff. Admittedly, not every specialist was enthusiastic about the new service.

Over time one needs to have a conversation with as many employees of the hospital as is possible. Each unit and each employee has different views and ideas which need to be addressed. Furthermore, these may all change over time. Conversations at this level help to change ideas and views about problems, and to engage people as appropriate.

A modest, 'one-down' approach with colleagues and managers seems to elicit the least resistance from them. As far as is possible, the consultant should endeavour to present himself being in the process of learning and developing ideas. The effect is that one is less likely to be hindered in one's task even if some members of staff do not themselves endorse the views of the consultant.

STAFF STRESS
AND
INTERNAL CONSULTATION

Work in a hospital can be pleasurable, challenging and, at times, stressful. Work related stress is managed increasingly by providing for staff discussion and consultation groups. In these instances, psychologists, psychiatrists, social workers, psychotherapists and hospital chaplains are most likely to be involved in consultations to staff groups because of their training and experience in the management of interpersonal problems. Stress is most likely to arise from the following sources:

1. Unanticipated and stressful tasks, such as caring for young, dying patients; feeling unable to reassure patients about their condition; not having the skills to carry out a special task and having to counsel relatives of a patient in the context of confidentiality rules.

2. Management and organizational difficulties, such as poor communication between managers and staff when decisions that affect one or the other are being made; pressure at work to undertake more clinical or research work; insufficient and inadequate resources, and poor

supervision and support.

3. Personal issues, such as pressure from a spouse to change from a night to a day shift; over-identification with some patients and a breakdown of professional boundaries; difficulty in achieving a balance between time spent at home and time spent at work, and anxiety about acquiring an infection through a spouse who works in a hospital.

Some professionals might complain of 'burnout' and high levels of stress. This is most common in specialized units such as an intensive care, renal units, AIDS units and oncology units. Staff may reveal their stress in a number of ways including absenteeism, coming in late for meetings, low morale, becoming short tempered and an inability to make decisions or delegate responsibilities. 'Burnout' is most likely to arise where there is a discrepancy between the demands of a job and the ability of that staff number to fulfil those demands.

Consultation to professional staff provides an opportunity to prevent stress in the workplace and ameliorate its effects. The internal consultant needs to set up consultation meetings in much the same way as any other consultation in order to avoid the pitfalls inherent in not properly liaising with the referrer or defining the problem in the first instance. In our experience it is more likely to be a nurse or hospital manager who first identifies the need for a staff group. This has implications for the involvement and participation of their medical colleagues. This observation may lead to an initial idea that nurses and other non-medical staff may feel unsupported in their task while doctors may view it as appropriate to put themselves at some distance from emotional and interpersonal problems, both with colleagues and staff. For this reason careful thought has been given to the composition of a staff group, as well as rostering schedules, if attendance is to be maximized. Agreement must be reached as to who will provide clinical cover while the meeting takes place. It would be unusual for all members of a team or unit to be able to attend. Furthermore, provision has to be made for emergency and 'bleep' calls during the course of consultation.

Group consultation does not negate the need for sessions with individuals, with a focus on counselling or therapy for that person. Some hospitals provide for this within the organisation, such as through a staff counsellor or in the Occupational Health

Department. Special arrangements need to be made for staff counselling in the hospital because of problems of confidentiality. Some members of staff feel that it is a weakness to ask for psychological support. For this reason both the physical location of the counsellor and his professional status within the organisation would probably have a bearing on the course and outcome of the counselling. This is not to suggest that doctors must only be counselled by doctors, but that these issues are by no means insignificant in setting up counselling.

Special thought needs to be given to the situation in which the head of a unit or department serves as the consultant. This can impede in the objectives of the meetings as members of staff may feel reluctant to discuss problems which frankly might impede in their chances for promotion or affect relationships with colleagues. On the other hand, the absence of the head of the unit may prove a handicap insofar as important decisions cannot be reached and managerial authority is not forthcoming. Our preference is to use a consultant within the institution but outside of the unit, such as the hospital chaplain or a psychiatrist to act as a consultant.

Personal problems and situations in their home life may well have a bearing on stress levels and work performance of professionals. *It is important to keep in mind that when consulting to professionals, the task is to understand behaviour in the context of the professional work situation rather than in one's personal life.* This is a boundary which should be maintained. In all cases, the consultant should first obtain the permission of the consultee to discuss personal issues. The following is an example of how these boundaries between professional problems and work problems can be clarified in the course of consultation.

Nurse: We've had three deaths on the ward this week ... it feels dreadful coming to work in the evening ... I've known two of the patients for over three years.

Consultant: What support have you had for this?

Nurse: There's been so little time and because I'm on a late shift I don't get a chance to meet with the other staff.

Consultant: How do you understand that you have been affected in this way at this time?

Nurse: Actually, if my daughter weren't wetting her bed at night I might have more energy to face up to this.

Consultant: I see; what effect does this have on your work?

Nurse: I just loathe dealing with the incontinent patients. I usually get a student nurse in to remake the bed and this is not right because they're not meant to deal with patients in isolation units with this infection.

Consultant: So how can you go about getting more support for yourself?

Nurse: I'm thinking of speaking to the nursing officer and also arranging a few sessions with the hospital chaplain.

In this case, the consultant recognizes the implications for the nurse in her home life of her stress, but then examines the effect of this on her work rather than pursues the apparent problems at home. The focus is on the practical problem -solving and addressing support (or the lack thereof) in the professional hierarchy.

Groups of this kind may differ from other requests for consultation as the task may be on going and the arrangement may be to offer consultation over an indefinite period. This stems from a belief that stress is inherent in hospital work and that consultation is one way of addressing this. The contract and task of the group should be reviewed from time to time, particularly in view of 'perturbations' that may arise when a new member of staff joins the group. The internal consultant also needs to recognize that changes in management and working practice may also prompt a review of the consultation task and contract. The consultant must respond to evolving definitions of the task of the group, both from within and without. Consultation is better 'sold' to say managers as a strategy for helping with absenteeism and work performance rather than as a forum for discussing management problems.

A CONVERSATION
ABOUT
INTERNAL CONSULTATION

Case discussion and a review of our clinical work is an important feature of how we work as a team. It helps us to become observers to some of our work, to take a wider (and different) perspective, to become a cohesive professional group and to review our failures and successes in order to improve on our work. We also discuss some of the theories which influence and inform our practice. Some points we discuss are:

What are we doing that apparently makes a difference?

What could we be doing differently?

What sort of referrals are we getting and how are they being made?

What information from different parts of the hospital reflects on our conduct and performance?

What further information do we need?

If someone else were observing our group discussion, what might be their comments?

What special problems arise for us in consulting to a hospital of which we are a part?

The following is an excerpt from a discussion which the authors had about the last question which may illustrate some of the dilemmas of the internal consultant.

RB: I'd like us to think about the similarities and differences between consulting to a team or a system of which we are a part. As you know, I am employed to do clinical work in this hospital, and you to do clinical work and to manage. How then do we see the consultation task fitting into the work that we do?

RM: The work we do and the theoretical basis for what we do is all based on 'systemic thinking'. The way we work with individuals or families can be extrapolated for thinking about larger systems.

RB: To whom do we define ourselves as consultants? What I am asking is: what is the difference between clinical work and consultation work?

RM: The definition first comes from whomever defines the problem. But there has to be agreement about the consultation task. That is the first task in consultation.

RB: That also makes me think that perhaps we should be consulting each time we have a clinical case. In other words, we should be clarifying what our referrer wants of us before we accept a piece for clinical work.

RM: Each time you meet with a client or family, it is in a sense, a consultation. We decide whether there should be further consultation at the end of each meeting or session. Perhaps we only sometimes do 'therapy' as such, but we always consult.

RB: Yes, I would agree with that. I was just thinking, are there any special constraints on us in our particular setting? Given that we have a sense of loyalty to the institution of which we are a part, and that we are employed and paid by it, does this compromise us in any way? Does it impede in our task in any way? What are your views about this?

RM: I can only give you one example of this. At one stage in our haemophilia centre, the consultant wanted to consider employing a psychologist in the centre with me. My immediate reaction was how would I define the boundaries between what I do and what he does? Not being neutral, my first thoughts were "No, we can consult a psychologist if we need one". I suppose that is an example of not thinking before acting!

RB: That gives me the idea that perhaps there may be greater constraints on being 'neutral'. I suppose, professionally, we should always consider that the use of an external consultant unknown to the institution may help if there is a particular impasse or where we recognise that our lack of neutrality would impede in our consultation work.

RM: Yes, and when there is a problem of which one is part, it does help to discuss it with an outsider and maybe in this particular instance one really needed someone else to be asking the questions of me, such as: "If a psychologist were employed, what would be the most difficult thing for you? What might be easier for you?" and, "How would you handle any impasse between you?"

RB: We also have to think about the special message that may be given when the internal consultant asks for external consultation. It could also be a manifestation of the problem at a wider level. By this I mean the internal consultant looks to the external consultant to support him in his task. In other words, the lack of neutrality is carried over in making the referral to the consultant.

RM: So my question to you is, can one ever   be completely neutral, or is it ever desirable to be completely neutral?

RB: I prefer to answer the second part of your question. I think we have to recognise that there are constraints by virtue of the fact that we are paid to carry out a certain task in the hospital. If, in the course of our work, we feel that we cannot fulfil that task for whatever reason, it should be our clinical judgement which guides us to either employ an external consultant or to identify the constraints that we have in relation to the particular problem, and to feed this back to our managers. I don't think it is necessarily desirable nor possible to be completely neutral about anything at all. It's just like being in a family. One can never *simultaneously* view things from several perspectives. We have to recognise that we are 'editing' and organising what we see, and this in turn affects how we view things.

RM: And perhaps the prefix to all questions about problems is: "In my view at this time, this is how I see it."

RB: I agree. The structure, that is, the hospital, hardly changes over time. But the beliefs, the staff, the problems, and indeed the definition of problems, will keep evolving. For that reason, we should *keep on* asking questions, of ourselves, of our referrers, and of our managers who define our tasks in order to clarify ideas and beliefs.

SUMMARY AND
LEARNING POINTS

"That's the reason they're called lessons,"
the Gryphon remarked,
"because they lessen from day to day."
(Lewis Carroll)

Problems, whether they affect individuals or organizations, are at one level opportunities. They signal the possibility for change. As professionals working in a hospital, one may have the choice as to whether one first offers consultation before taking on a referral. Our preference is to first consult over a problem before taking on clinical responsibility for a case. In so doing, we feel we may be able to retain a more neutral view of the problem and ensure some level of flexibility in planning for change. Health care workers who consult within hospitals and offer a clinical service in the hospital may slip in and out of clinical consulting roles. Each clinical situation will be managed by different approaches and strategies and however, a number of guide-lines and conceptual ideas which can serve to guide the internal consultant:

*   Problems are inevitable in organisations, and not all of them require consultation. Where there is an apparent lack of agreement about a problem or around its solution, consultation maybe indicated. Seeking advice from a colleague about managing a case can also be the start of consultation. The internal consultant in the hospital setting

does not take on clinical responsibility for a case or the problem, this remains with the consultee.

* Professionals may work as clinicians or consultants at different times in the hospital; they are rarely full-time consultants. On the other hand, every clinical case can engender some consultation work. Whenever possible, referrals or requests for advice should be preceded by a discussion about

a. what is expected from the consultant/colleague,

b. what feedback over the case is required,

c. what are the criteria for closing the case, or the end of the problem.

* The tasks of the consultant are varied, but include some of the following:

a. bringing forth the problem in usable language,

b. determining who has defined a problem and how it has been defined,

c. retaining a level of neutrality in relation to problem and decisions,

d. placing the responsibility for problem solving with those who define the problem,

e. eliciting the assumptions about people and actions that seem to maintain the problem,

f. addressing the relationship between consultants and colleagues and the implications this has for their work in the hospital.

A number of ideas and approaches can help facilitate effective internal consultation. These include some of the following:

* The greatest fears of the consultee in relation to his task (or

inability to fulfil it) should be addressed at some point in the consultation.

* Change and interventions have a ripple effect on other parts of the hospital.

* The consultant should secure the permission of those higher up in hierarchy in order to facilitate their task.

* A 'one-down' position and a curious stance in relation to problems is less threatening to colleagues.

* Address colleagues by their professional titles (until invited to do otherwise). Conservative dress style (suits, ties and so on) are a particular communication to colleagues in hospitals!

* Goals should be small, and attainable. Change is often slow and incremental, or it can be sudden and unaccountable.

The transition to becoming a consultant may be marked by periods of confusion about one's role; " What is being asked of me here? How do I deal with the problem, without telling my colleagues what to do? Is this a referral?" We sometimes respond to these questions by arranging for external consultation. This helps us to reflect on our task as a consultant and on our evolving different positions in the hospital in relation to other teams and departments. Consultation is therefore potentially of value in any situation where professionals (clinical and managerial) experience uncertainty, unpredictability and change in a hospital setting.

EXERCISES FOR INITIATING CONSULTATION

Both clinical experience and seniority in the organisation are likely to lead to requests for consultation in the hospital setting. Consultation skills can be developed by attending one of the growing number of consultation courses now offered. One can also gain familiarity with some of the associated skills through clinical work and in the course of accepting new referrals. A few examples of consultation exercises have been listed below. These exercises are based on situations which we have dealt with or set up in the course of our 'progression' towards becoming internal consultants. They are mostly exercises which can be initiated in the course of one's work and do not require special training sessions or too much extra time with patients or colleagues. The exercises are best tackled with a colleague, with whom one can develop and share ideas. In addition, colleagues can act as consultants to one another in the course of managing some of the problems that may arise in the course of tackling some of the exercises.

1.   The next time a clinical case is referred to you, arrange to spend five or ten minutes with the referrer in order to discuss;

a) what he/she expects of you in relation to the case

b) what feedback he/she would find helpful.

2.   Arrange a joint meeting between yourself and one of your main referrers in which you see a patient/client/family together. Define it an opportunity for you to learn from him or her. Use some of the post-session review to discuss a few advantages and limitations of working together over some cases.

3.   In the absence of having a team to help you in your consultation work, describe at least two other views of the problems you identified and consider how you might present these to your consultee.

4.   How would you describe the difference between consultation and liaison to a trainee?

5.   In reviewing a case; what one thing in each case would you have had to do differently in order to be seen to be more

      *   prescriptive ?

      *   judgmental ?

6.   Assume that you have been asked by your line manager to offer a consultation to a group of junior members of staff. How might you go about this in relation to

      *   the line manager?

      *   the group to whom you are expected to consult?

7.   Discuss with a colleague some of the advantages and disadvantages of only undertaking consultation work or only practising as a clinician.

8.   Practice consultation interviewing skills with a colleague with whom you have arranged to discuss a clinical case. After ten minutes ask your colleague to tell you what he or she found helpful and unhelpful in your interview and to comment on your interviewing style. Swap over roles so

that you can experience being consulted to and after feedback to your colleague. Then consider how you might conduct a consultation interview as a team with another member of your department or unit as a consultee.

FURTHER READING

ABOUT CONSULTATION,
FAMILY-SYSTEMS THEORY
AND HOSPITAL SYSTEMS

Burnham,J. (1986) **Family Therapy.** *London. Tavistock Publications.*

Campbell,D. & Draper, R (Eds.) (1985) **Applications of Systemic Family Therapy.** *London. Grune & Stratton.*
Campbell,D.,Draper,R. & Huffington,C. (1989) **Second Thoughts on the Theory and Practice of the Milan Approach to Family Therapy.** *London. Karnac.*
Campbell,D., Draper,R. & Huffington,C. (1989) **A Systemic Approach to Consultation.** *London. Karnac.*

Hoffman,L, (1981) **Foundations of Family Therapy.** *New York. Basic Books.*

Imber-Black,E. (1988) **Families and Larger Systems.** *New York. Guilford Press.*

Miller,R. & Bor,R. (1988) **AIDS: A Guide to Clinical Counselling.** *London. Science Press.*

Quinnett,P. (1989) **On Becoming a Health and Human Services**

Manager. *New York. Continuum.*

Selvini Palazzoli,M.,Anolli,L.,DiBlasio *et.al.* (1986) **The Hidden Games of Organizations.** *New York. Pantheon Books.*

Watzlawick,P., Weakland,L. & Fisch,R. (1974) **Change.** *New York. Norton.*
Wynne,L., McDaniel,S. & Weber,T. (1986) **Systems Consultation.** *New York. Guilford Press.*